Show
HORSES

by Margaret Fetty

Consultant: Clay A. Cavinder, Ph.D.

New York, New York

Credits

Cover and Title Page, John Terence Turner/Getty Images; 4, © Kit Houghton Photography; 5, © Kit Houghton Photography; 6, © Kit Houghton Photography; 7, © Kit Houghton Photography; 8, © Kit Houghton Photography; 9, © Johnny Johnston. Photo Courtesy of Sheila Varian/Varian Arabians; 10, © Bob Langrish Photography; 11, © Kit Houghton Photography; 12, © Erich Lessing/Art Resource, NY; 13, © Roland Schlager/epa/Corbis; 14, © Bob Langrish/Animals Animals Earth Scenes; 15, © Mike Ferrara Photography; 16, © Kit Houghton Photography; 17, © Kit Houghton Photography; 18, © Kit Houghton Photography; 19, © Kit Houghton Photography; 20, © Sylvia Loch. Reprinted with permission from the book Invisible Riding; 21, © A. Inden/zefa/Corbis; 22, © Kit Houghton Photography; 23, Photo Courtesy of Suzanne Perkins; 24, © Kit Houghton Photography; 25, © Dr. Wiley/Equi-Center Veterinary Hospital; 26, © Kit Houghton Photography; 27, © Kit Houghton Photography; 29TL, © Arco Images/Alamy; 29TR, © Juniors Bildarchiv/Alamy; 29BL, © Juniors Bildarchiv/Alamy; 29BR, © Arco Images/Alamy.

Publisher: Kenn Goin
Project Editor: Lisa Wiseman
Creative Director: Spencer Brinker
Photo Researcher: Elaine Soares
Design: Stacey May

Library of Congress Cataloging-in-Publication Data

Fetty, Margaret.
  Show horses / by Margaret Fetty.
    p. cm. — (Horse power)
  Includes bibliographical references and index.
  ISBN-13: 978-1-59716-399-6 (library binding)
  ISBN-10: 1-59716-399-6 (library binding)
 1. Show horses—Juvenile literature. 2. Horse shows—Juvenile literature. I. Title. II. Series: Horse power (Series)

  SF295.185.F48 2007
  798.2—dc22
                          2006030264

For more information, write to Bearport Publishing Company, Inc., 101 Fifth Avenue, Suite 6R, New York, New York 10003. Printed in the United States of America.

10 9 8 7 6 5 4 3 2 1

Contents

An Olympic Ride

It was the 2000 Summer Olympic Games. The Australian **equestrian** team was leading Great Britain by just a few points in the **three-day event**. Andrew Hoy and his horse, Darien Powers, entered the **ring**. Hoy, the last Australian rider, knew that they needed to jump well in order to win.

Andrew Hoy and Darien Powers

Hoy and his horse began the **course**. They easily cleared the first few **fences**. Everything was going well until they got to fence 8. As Darien Powers jumped, two **rails** fell and clattered into the dirt. Then, at fence 11, another rail fell. There were only two fences left. Darien Powers would have to clear both of them in order to win.

Andrew Hoy and Darien Powers complete a jump in the 2000 Summer Olympic Games in Sydney, Australia.

The fences that horses jump are often made with colorful poles, boards, bricks, or shrubs.

Going for the Gold

Hoy steadied Darien Powers. They cleared fence 12. The last fence was just steps ahead.

Hoy gripped Darien Powers with his legs. The horse leaped up. His back legs pushed the two of them high into the air. They sailed over fence 13 and raced to finish the course. The Australian team won the gold medal!

The Australian three-day event team celebrates their gold medal win in the 2000 Summer Olympic Games.

Even before winning at the Olympics, Darien Powers was a successful show horse. He had **competed** in many events around the world. Like other show horses, Darien Powers had speed, strength, and courage. Yet he was also calm and had good manners. Together, he and Andrew Hoy made a winning team.

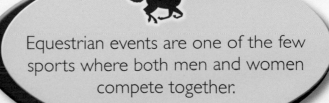

Equestrian events are one of the few sports where both men and women compete together.

Showing Off

There are three different kinds of show horses. **Performance horses,** along with their riders, are judged on their skills. The animals walk**, trot**, and **canter**. Some jump over fences or run long distances quickly. Darien Powers was a special performance horse. He was good at all these skills.

Darien Powers shows off his skills as he splashes through the water during the Royal International Horse Show.

Some show horses don't need to rely on their skills. They are judged on their looks. The winner is considered the best of his **breed**.

Other horses are perfect for **equitation** because of their smooth trot and canter. Their easy rhythm helps a rider sit still in the **saddle**. Riders are judged on their style and control of the horse.

Huckleberry Bey, a famous Arabian horse, is a breed show winner.

In a breed event, horses are shown without saddles.

Classes

During a show, performance horses compete in different **classes**. In jumping class, horses leap over fences, trying not to knock them down. In **dressage** events, they perform a **pattern** of steps. In other classes, horses only walk, trot, and canter around a ring.

Dressage is similar to ballet for horses. The most experienced dressage horses can even canter in place.

Andrew Hoy and Darien Powers ride in the most challenging class—the three-day event. On the first day, they ride dressage. On the second day, the pair competes in a cross-country race. They run through water and leap over **obstacles** as they complete a 14-mile (23-km) course. Finally, Hoy and Darien Powers jump fences in a ring on the third day.

Riders must wear a crash helmet and a protective vest during a cross-country event. This equipment helps keep them safe if they fall off the horse.

Andrew Hoy and Darien Powers jump over an obstacle during the cross-country part of a three-day event.

A Military Start

Many horse show events got their start in the military. Hundreds of years ago, soldiers began riding horses in battles. To prepare the animals, soldiers trained their horses to run long distances at high speeds. They had the animals practice jumping over fences so they could get used to obstacles on a battlefield. Sometimes, the soldiers competed with each other to see whose horse had the best skills. These contests led to modern-day cross-country and jumping events.

Soldiers and their horses in battle

During battles, soldiers had to use their hands to hold weapons. Their legs and body positions were used to guide their horses.

Dressage is also based on military practices. When not fighting, soldiers trained their horses to move in different patterns. Then they performed the movements as a group in parades. While dressage riders now compete alone, they still use some of the military steps.

The Lipizzaners, trained at the Spanish Riding School in Vienna, Austria, are famous for their dressage movements and their graceful jumps.

Show Horse Qualities

Different breeds of show horses have certain qualities that help them compete in various events. For example, Trakehners are often used in dressage events. These horses are smart. They can quickly learn different steps. They are also graceful and can perform movements with style.

Trakehners come in many colors, including gray, chestnut, or black.

A jumping horse needs powerful muscles and strong legs. Hanoverians make popular jumpers. While they have lots of energy, they can also remain calm in the ring.

For equitation, Arabians are the perfect choice. These lively and intelligent horses have great speed. They are also easy to ride because they have a smooth rhythm.

Arabian horses and riders often compete in costumes from the past to celebrate the history of the horse.

Show horses have long, thin legs and narrow chests and backs. Their bodies are small, which allow them to move quickly and easily.

From the Beginning

All breeds of show horses have to learn basic skills and manners. For **foals**, training begins after they are born. Right away, they are touched or handled by different people. This helps them learn to trust humans. During their first year, young horses are led around the stable. They are taught commands, such as "walk" and "stop."

Trainers walk around with the foals so that the animals can learn the different sights and sounds of the farm.

A filly is a female horse that is two years old or younger. A male horse that is two years old or younger is called a colt.

By the age of one, many horses are **lunged** in a ring. This exercise helps them build strong muscles. Then a **trainer** slowly gets them used to a **bridle**. Finally, between the ages of two and three, most horses are wearing a saddle. They are now ready for someone to ride them!

To lunge a horse, a trainer uses a long rope to make the animal walk, trot, and canter in a circle.

Getting into Sports

When a horse is about four years old, a trainer watches him to see what skills he has. The trainer will determine which events the animal will be good at. For example, a horse that learns quickly might do dressage. One that lifts his knees high into the air could compete in equitation events.

A trainer watches his horse as the animal moves around the ring.

Once the trainer identifies these skills, she works with the horse to develop them. For horses that jump, trainers first lay poles on the ground. The animals walk and trot over them. Soon, the poles are raised off the ground for the horses to jump over. Finally, the animals leap over fences of different heights and widths.

A horse trotting over raised poles

In jumping classes, the fences are built so they can be knocked down. However, in cross-country events, the obstacles are solid and cannot be moved.

Time to Ride

After basic training, a horse is ready for a rider. At this point, a riding instructor, such as Sylvia Loch, can help. Loch teaches the rider how to use her body and legs to guide the animal. She also teaches her how to work with the horse. Soon, the horse and rider begin to trust each other. They learn to work together as a team.

Sylvia Loch (left) trains with a rider.

After several months, a rider learns the moods of her horse. She can tell when the horse is happy, playful, or grumpy. She also knows how the animal might act during those times, too. Likewise, a horse learns to understand how her teammate feels. A horse is calmer with a happy rider and will perform better in a show.

Horses eat grass, grain, hay, and carrots.

Horses have a sixth sense. They seem to know when the weather is about to change. They also know if danger is near.

Showtime!

At last, a horse and rider are ready to compete in a show. Riders can be of any age or skill level. The best ones go to the Olympics or the World Equestrian Games. However, a team must be invited to compete in these important shows. To be included, they need winning scores from other competitions.

In most classes, riders wear a dark jacket and light-colored riding **breeches**. They also wear black boots and a velvet helmet.

Suzanne Perkins is a show judge. She looks at the horses' bodies, manners, and movements. Perkins also notices how well the riders and horses work together. Then she gives each team a score. Depending on the event, the winning partners get a blue ribbon or, like Andrew Hoy and Darien Powers, a gold medal!

Suzanne Perkins (left), United States Equestrian Federation (USEF) licensed judge (Arabian, Andalusian, Friesian, and Western Divisions), during a show in Canada

Healing Horses

Horses can get hurt just like human athletes. Leg and hoof injuries are common. Horses can step on a stone and bruise the soft part on the inside of their hooves. They may hurt a muscle, too. These injuries can cause horses to be **lame**. They will have trouble walking and will need to rest until they heal.

To keep a horse's hooves healthy, riders use a hoof pick to pull out rocks and dirt.

Sometimes, a sick or injured horse will visit Dr. Michael Wiley, an **equine veterinarian**. Dr. Wiley listens to the horse's heartbeat and breathing. Then he takes the horse's temperature. Dr. Wiley may use an X-ray machine to look at the bones and muscles inside the animal. If necessary, he will perform an operation to help the horse get better.

In the three-day event, a veterinarian checks each horse after cross-country racing and before jumping. If the doctor feels that the animal is not healthy, the team has to drop out.

Dr. Wiley checks a patient's teeth.

A Winning Team

To stay healthy and strong, a show horse team spends many hours training. The rider exercises the horse to keep his muscles strong. They practice the movements of the sport, such as jumping or dressage steps, to keep their skills sharp. As they work, the pair also strengthens their trust and friendship.

Andrew Hoy trains horses 7 days a week for 12 hours each day.

A strong partnership is important in forming a winning team. A horse and rider often spend years together. Andrew Hoy and Darien Powers competed as a team for eight years. They won many awards, including Olympic gold medals. A show horse is not only a teammate, but is also considered a best friend!

Andrew Hoy celebrates his Olympic win in 2000.

Andrew Hoy has won three gold medals in the Olympic Games. Two of these medals were won while he was riding Darien Powers.

Just the Facts

- Hunt Seat is the style of riding most often seen in shows. The horse wears a small, close-fitting saddle. Riders lift themselves partly out of the saddle when the horse runs or jumps. This position allows the horse to have better balance and move more quickly.

- When mistakes are made in a jumping class, a rider gets points called faults. Errors include knocking down a rail, refusing to jump an obstacle, taking too long on the course, or having a rider fall off. The team with the least number of faults wins.

- Until 1952, only male military officers were allowed to compete in the Olympic Games. That same year, Liz Hartel, who did not have the use of her legs, won the silver medal in dressage.

- Vaulting is a sport in which a person or team performs gymnastic and dance movements on the back of a horse. A trainer holds a lunge line and keeps the horse moving in a circle. The vaulters jump, flip, and do handstands as the horse moves.

Show Horses

Arabian

Hanoverian

Trakehner

Oldenburg

Glossary

breeches (BRICH-iz) pants a rider wears that are knee-length or longer

breed (BREED) a type of a certain animal

bridle (BRYE-duhl) a strap that fits around a horse's head and mouth that is used to guide him

canter (KAN-tur) to run at a speed between a trot and a gallop

classes (KLAS-uhz) events in a show in which a group of horses or riders have one skill or quality that is being judged

competed (kuhm-PEE-tuhd) tried to win an event or contest

course (KORSS) a set path

dressage (druh-SAHJ) a riding style in which horses perform a series of moves

equestrian (i-KWESS-tree-uhn) having to do with horseback riding

equine veterinarian (EE-kwine *vet*-ur-uh-NER-ee-uhn) a doctor who treats horses

equitation (*ek*-wuh-TAY-shuhn) the act of riding on horseback; riders are judged on style

fences (FEN-sez) obstacles made of poles, plants, stones, or bricks

foals (FOHLZ) newborn horses that are still being nursed by their mothers

lame (LAYM) having trouble moving

lunged (LUHNJD) a way to exercise a horse in which a trainer stands in the middle of the ring holding a long rope and makes the animal move in a circle around him

obstacles (OB-stuh-kuhlz) things that block a path

pattern (PAT-urn) repeating a set of movements or actions

performance horses (pur-FOR-muhnss HORSS-iz) types of horses that have athletic skills

rails (RAYLZ) the poles that are part of a fence

ring (RING) an area shaped like a circle or an oval, where horses and riders practice and compete

saddle (SAD-uhl) a seat for a rider that fits on top of the horse's back

three-day event (THREE-DAY i-VENT) the part of a horse show in which riders participate in three different types of classes over three days

trainer (TRAY-nur) a person who teaches horses how to do different things

trot (TROT) to move faster than a walk but slower than a canter

Bibliography

Parker, Jane. *The Fantastic Book of Horses.* Brookfield, CT: Copper Beech Books (1997).

Pickeral, Tamsin. *The Encyclopedia of Horses and Ponies.* Cologne, Germany: Parragon Plus (2001).

www.olympic.org/uk/sports/programme/index_uk.asp?SportCode=EQ

www.times-olympics.co.uk/archive/equess19o.html

Read More

Hayden, Kate. *Horse Show.* New York: DK Publishing, Inc. (2001).

Kimball, Cheryl. *Horse Showing for Kids.* North Adams, MA: Storey Publishing (2004).

U.S. Olympic Committee. *A Basic Guide to Equestrian.* Irvine, CA: Griffin Publishing Group (2001).

White-Thomson, Stephen. *On Horseback.* Morristown, NJ: Silver Burdett (1981).

Learn More Online

To learn more about show horses, visit
www.bearportpublishing.com/HorsePower

Index

About the Author

Margaret Fetty has written numerous children's books.
She lives in Austin, Texas, where she enjoys running and biking.